INVASION REVEALED

Healing Alcoholism, Mental Illness, & Drug Addiction

I0558405

Nancy Lynne Harris M.A.

HEALING ALCOHOLISM
MENTAL ILLNESS & DRUG
ADDICTION

INVASION REVEALED

Nancy Lynne Harris, M.A.

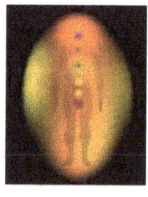

ARPress
ILLUMINATING IDEAS.
EMPOWERING VOICES.

ARPress
45 Dan Rd, Suite 36
Canton MA 02021
Hotline: 1(800) 220-7660
Fax: 1(855) 752-6001

Ordering Information:

Quantity sales. Special discounts are available on
quantity purchases by corporations, associations,
and others. For details, contact the publisher at
the address above.

Printed in the United States of America.

Library of Congress Control Number
ISBN-13:   Paperback   979-8-89389-042-6
                eBook   979-8-89389-043-3

Rev. date: 03/25/2019

Dedicated to my dad Jack, an alcoholic,
who taught me compassion for others
who find no help –
even when they look for it in the traditional
places.

FOREWORD

Alcoholism, drug addiction, mental illness, Alzheimer's, and other illnesses are caused from the individual's unintentional neglect and/or ignorance of the spirit nature of the Self. Millions of people worldwide have these problems, and many succumb to them.

People may be helped, or subdued, by medicine to some degree, if the individual is willing to take prescription drugs every day for the rest of his life, but statistics prove that medical help is not the answer to healing dysfunction. Even so, our customs change slowly, and thousands suffer and die while we wait for a different approach to healing.

Professionals who offer help need to understand the spiritual problem that is causing the dysfunction. Sick people must be trained to think differently about themselves before they can recover. When the individual is trained to change from within by improving his love/hate relationship with himself, real healing becomes possible. Recovery happens *only* if the individual is willing to work on changing and improving his or her attitudes and negative opinions about the Self, (the *I AM* part of you). If these individuals already had knowledge of how to care for the Self successfully, they would not be sick. Through spiritual training, self-correction, and change from within, they can heal.

We can recover from dysfunctional problems by learning how we operate as *thinking* Spirit Beings and by consciously recognizing our responsibility to the *correct use*, rather than continued misuse, of the Spirit Energy we are made of.

Many centuries ago Jesus showed us how to overcome what he called 'the prince of this world.' What he demonstrated may not be the answer you would prefer, but his words and actions perfectly explain what is *still* causing dysfunction and chaos in our lives today.

If parents across the world would begin to teach their *little* children to love the essence and substance of the Self with all their heart, soul, and mind, these children would grow up so full of love (rather than full of dysfunctional problems), in time our world would be transformed. The lesson we all have yet to learn and demonstrate is the triumphant power of Self-Love.

Climbing up, reach for the sky

Higher than high, see – I can fly

You say you can't! Did you ever try?

~ Nancy Lynne Harris

Chapter One

INVASION REVEALED

Alcoholism, drug addiction, depression, and Alzheimer's are all caused by the same thing—the individual's unintentional neglect and ignorance of the Spirit nature of the Self. We live in a spiritual universe that we do not recognize as such, even though we are in the midst of a fierce spiritual battle that has been going on for centuries. Every time another person commits suicide or otherwise dies from dysfunction, the enemy has scored another victory. We, in our ignorance, just go on in the same old way, allowing this to happen over and over again. Winning spiritual battles requires conscious Self-awareness and willingness to change the failing status quo.

Complete healing from dysfunction is accomplished only when the individual is willing to change from within and work on improving his Love/Hate relationship with the Self. We all know that dysfunctional illnesses cannot be healed with medicine. We must consciously recognize our responsibility for the *correct use*, rather than misuse, of the Light Energy we are each made of as Spirit-beings.

One day I was having lunch with three ladies. The lady sitting directly across from me said she worked in a mental institution as a psychiatrist. She was obviously very proud of her status. When someone mentioned to her that I am an energy healer, she said to me in a disparaging tone, "Oh, you do woo-woo!" I said "No!" I was surprised by her condescending attitude, and I wanted to say, "What I do works, and I do not incarcerate anyone," but I did not say anything else. If your mind is closed, you will not save people's lives no matter how many graduate degrees you may have. We all know our mental health system is failing. Albert Einstein said, "The definition of insanity is doing something over and over in the same way and expecting different results."

According to current national statistics, more than 75 percent of American families are now considered dysfunctional, with substance abuse addictions involving alcohol, drugs, and untreated mental illness. More teens are killed by alcohol than by all illegal drugs combined. Millions of people who drink are mentally ill.

A few years ago I ordered a catalog from the United States Printing Office in Washington, D.C., listing all the psychiatric providers and mental institutions in the country. They sent me a catalog as large as a Manhattan telephone directory. Why are there still millions of people with addictions and thousands of suicides each year if all these qualified psychiatric professionals are providing their services? Obviously, something is wrong here. Based on their current level of understanding, medically trained professionals try to solve spiritual illnesses in physical ways that do not work.

In depression, the doctor may give you pills to help you cope or sleep, but there is no magic pill to heal dysfunction. Even if you enter a treatment facility where you come out clean and sober, the underlying cause of your problem is still present in your mind. Some patients are confined to mental institutions where they are sedated daily with drugs, sometimes for many years, with little chance of recovery. Suffering patients may even agree to have electric shocks and other archaic mistreatments administered by well-meaning people who do not understand the invisible cause of dysfunction. When we find that medically-trained professionals have done all they can and we are still ill, it's no wonder we look for other modalities of healing. With millions of people suffering from dysfunction, we find the diagnosis of "medically incurable" unacceptable.

My dad Jack was a gentle, kind man, a chronic alcoholic, and a member of Alcoholics Anonymous. During my childhood, I remember him lying in bed sick and the doctor coming to our home many times to give him barbiturates to calm his nerves and a shot to help him sleep. Dad was so tormented, after many years of trying to recover from alcoholism, that he took prescription barbiturates while he was drinking, and his fourth wife found him face down on the floor, dead at age fifty-two. There was no relief for this poor man even though he tried many times to find help.

When I was about 8 years old, I saw Dad sitting on the side of his bed one day. He said, "Nancy, come over here and sit down beside me. I want to share something with you." He opened the bedside table drawer, took out a copy of the Serenity Prayer and began to read it out loud to me.

God grant me the serenity

to accept the things I cannot change,

the courage to change the things I can,

and the wisdom to know the difference.

(attr. to Reinhold Niebuhr)

I will always appreciate my dad's gift to me that day. I wish with all my heart that I could say to him now, "Dad, I know what's causing your problem. I can help you get well!" He would be so grateful.

For many years the belief has been that dysfunctional people are abnormal. This belief creates so much shame and embarrassment that many suffering people do not seek help at all. How can anyone say that we are abnormal when there are millions of dysfunctional people? We have become the normal. We are the victims who are caught up in the dark energy affecting this world. Now it is time for us to come into the Light where we can see what is really happening so we can all get well.

The alcoholics or addicts that you might know could be your son, your daughter, your wife or yourself, and you desperately need help. My son Michael was killed in a car accident a few days after his 18th birthday. My son Jeffrey hanged himself because of depression. He was 48 with a wife that he loved and two teenaged daughters. When I divorced my ex-husband Ray, he was experiencing chemical blackouts from daily alcoholic poisoning and many other health problems. It was impossible for me to help him, because he wouldn't listen to me. My attempts were fruitless. It is heartbreaking to divorce someone you love, but marriage requires cooperation.

I lost my family, but I will do my best to help you save yours. I know now that the purpose of my life is to teach you what is really happening in dysfunction so you and your family can get well. You can overcome addictions and even depression if you understand what the unseen underlying problem is. I will tell you how to recover from alcoholism, drug addiction, and depression based on Jesus' teaching. I know from my own experience that His method of healing works perfectly when understood.

The event that changed my life was Michael's death. He was driving home at 6 A.M. from a teenage drug party on a curving river road when he crashed our truck into a power pole that broke in half, fell across the truck, and killed him.

Mike began using drugs with his friends at age 14, and Ray and I had tried everything we knew—from doctors to counselors—to help him quit with no success. As a responsible mother, I blamed myself for his death. I began to hate myself intensely. You just don't lose your children. Over the next 8 years I experienced chronic depression. In depression you're dealing with constant mental torment. There is *no* peace in your mind.

One of the counselors I saw sent me to a psychiatrist who prescribed various medications—Amitriptyline, Lithium, Mellaril and Xanax. These medicines caused so many side effects that I chose to stop taking them, except for Xanax. Port wine and Xanax were the *only* things that ever gave me any mental relief. After 8 years of doctors, counseling, and medicines, my chronic depression had not improved at all, and my inner voice was encouraging me to commit suicide.

At that point, one morning I decided to do something I had never done before. I remember that I had painted my fingernails bright red to help me remember whose life I was trying to save. I could hardly concentrate on anything, because of the screaming voices in my mind. So, I sat down on my couch, covered my eyes with my hands, and looked inward for the first time in my life. I said, "What the hell is going on in here?"

I instantly saw 5 ghost-like creatures moving around in my mental space, seemingly right behind my eyes. They appeared to be planning their next treacherous maneuver to use on me, but I had taken them by surprise. One of these creatures turned his head and looked straight at me. Then they all scurried to hide in the dark edges of my mental space, and my mind went black, as if they had turned out the lights. In a state of extreme mental turmoil, I reasoned that this must be what Jesus meant by evil spirits. From that moment on I knew that my mental space had been invaded.

Jesus encountered a wild man who lived

among the tombs. Night and day he was

crying, and cutting himself with stones.

Jesus said, What is your name? He

answered, My name is Legion for we

are many.   Mark 5:9

Webster's Dictionary defines the word *legion* as "an army of 5,000 - 6,000 foot soldiers."

Jesus commanded, Come out of the man!

The Legion of evil spirits pleaded with

Jesus. They begged Him to send them into

the swine that were grazing on a

nearby hillside. Jesus said, Come Out!

And the evil spirits entered into the

herd of swine that ran violently down a

steep hill into the sea and were

drowned. When the invaders were gone,

the wild man was in his right mind.

Luke 8:30

In this story Jesus tells us exactly how to heal dysfunction. **There never was anything wrong with this man's mind. His mental space had been invaded by evil spirits (demons), and his mind had been possessed.** (According to *Webster*, the word *possession* means, "to lose control of yourself.")

I decided to use Jesus' method of healing on myself, since I was 8 years into this illness and nothing else was working. I reasoned that Jesus conversed with the intruders, and if I could hear them screaming at me, they could probably hear me screaming at them. I began yelling at them, "GET THE HELL OUT OF MY SPACE!" They were trying hard to get me to commit suicide, but I always chose not to take the action.

In addition to commanding them to get out, I began to say out loud, **"I BELIEVE IN MYSELF,"** and they began to loudly object. They wanted to keep me under their control, so I said to them,

I LOVE MYSELF TO THE DEPTH,

BREADTH, AND HEIGHT OF MY BEING.

I DISSOLVE THE NEED FOR

THE NEGATIVE VOICE.

By saying this, I was beginning to reverse my Self-hatred to Self-Love, and this began to make a BIG difference in the way I felt. In so doing, I went against what my dear well-meaning mother had taught me as a child. When I was 8 years old, s*he taught me **not** to love myself, because she said it was conceited.*

In 2010, Mother died of Alzheimer's. In Alzheimer's your mind is completely captured by demons. They maim and kill zillions of us that way every year. Of course, nobody blames it on demonic invasion for lack of Self-Love!

At the time, when I told my counselor that I was yelling at those creatures in my mind and telling them to get out, the counselor said, "Don't do that! Don't do that!" I guess she thought I was just imagining the whole thing. By continuing to do it Jesus' way rather than the counselor's way, I got well. What I learned in those 8 years of depression is that two psychiatrists and two counselors could not help me at all, even though one of the counselors told me that I had come to see her 49 times! If I had continued to do it the medical way, I would be dead. No one "out there" can heal you from depression. You are the *only one* who can make that difference for yourself.

From the day that I looked inward and saw the invaders, I began monitoring everything that was going on in my mind and consciously reversing my hateful thoughts about my-Self to loving thoughts. If you want to get well, you must change the way you think about your-Self from within your own mind to at least 51 percent positive.

LOVE YOURSELF WITH ALL YOUR

HEART, SOUL, AND MIND

EVERY MINUTE OF EVERY DAY.

IT IS THE WAY TO GET WELL.

During my illness, my hatred for myself over Michael's death was so intense that the word *hate* seemed to regenerate itself in my mind automatically. I could not think of a word that began with "h" (like *hope*) because my mind would turn the word into the word *hate*. I finally spoke directly to the word *hate* and used sexually explicit words to dispel it from my mind so it could no longer use my Spiritual Energy to reproduce itself. I said:

HATE IS GUTLESS, IMPOTENT, DISEMBOWELED AND PERMANENTLY STERILE WITHIN ME.

This worked perfectly to stop that word from regenerating itself in my mind. I began to consciously hold the word *Love* in my mind, which I had never done before in my life. By thinking the word *Love*, I *stopped* the course of my depression, but by thinking *Self-Love*, I *reversed* the negative flow of my Creative Energy, and I knew for certain I was getting well. To heal any illness, you *must* reverse your negative feelings. You cannot fool the Spiritual Energy that empowers your body. It is yours to control. It always reads and reflects your true feelings, no matter what you say to the contrary.

As I continued to think *I Love My-Self*, I was feeling better every day because I was thinking about my-Self in a new positive way. By thinking Self-Love, I was driving the invaders out of my mental space. As creatures of darkness, demons cannot live in an atmosphere of Self-Love, because when you think the word *Love*, it brightens the auric light that surrounds your body, so they are forced leave. We each have an auric light, which is a radiating, luminous glowing energy composed of beautiful rainbow colors surrounding your body. Your aura can clearly be seen if you are photographed with special computer software.

One night near the end of my recovery as I was lying in bed with my eyes closed, I observed a long procession of creatures (demons) dressed in black hooded cloaks carrying lighted candles, moving in single file going downward, leaving my mental space,

9

as if they were attending a formal funeral procession. But I knew it wasn't *my* funeral; it was theirs. I had won. After they were gone, my mind became so quiet that I was experiencing complete mental peace. It took me 8 months of persistent positive thinking to achieve my wellness from the day I first observed them. I was owning and protecting my inner mental spirit space for the first time in my life. I had proved that we, as Beings of Light, are more powerful than demons, as creatures of darkness, and *we* can control them, just as Jesus controlled them. They **had** to follow my command to get out of my space, and they could not stay in an atmosphere of Self-Love, because there was too much Light!

James Van Praagh, the famous medium, says in his book, *Ghosts Among Us*, "Individuals in an inebriated state are susceptible to ghostly attachment because alcohol depletes their protective auric field." He adds, "You would be shocked to know that many people who behave in horrific ways are being impressed or even possessed by dark and unevolved entities. They drain your energy and cause you to suffer accidents, injuries, and other misfortunes. Any form of chronic poor health can be a sign of ghostly attachment."

Drinking alcohol or using drugs creates portals (or what I call "space doors") in the luminous skin surrounding your auric field, enabling unevolved beings who live in dark immaterial mental space to enter your individual auric field. These are dark entities who have lost the auric light *that you are made of*, so they enter your mental space through these openings, or "space doors," that the alcohol and drugs create, and feed off your auric light energy. If you have an addiction, your mental spirit space has been invaded by these dark entities known as evil spirits or demons.

Dysfunction does NOT really classify as an illness, and there is really nothing wrong with your mind. This is why medicine fails to heal it. The mental space *where your words form* has been invaded, and you are under attack.

In her book, *Fallen Angels Among Us, What You Need to Know,* Elizabeth Claire Prophet talks about these demons and calls them "extra evil." She says they are making a mockery of the paradise God created and intended for us here on earth.

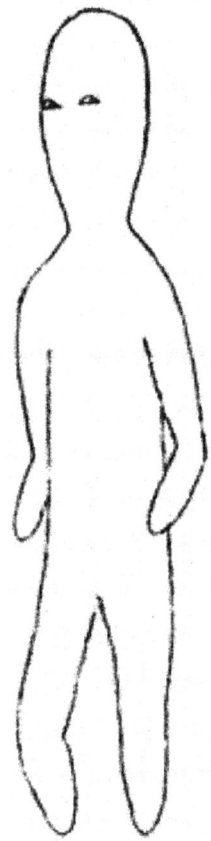

Evil Spirit

The ONLY thing that matters to you during a demonic invasion is that you find relief from the intense mental torment they create in your mind. It doesn't matter how much you love your wife, your husband, or your children. All that matters to you is that you get relief. Usually alcohol or hard drugs are the only substances that numb you enough to provide any alleviation from the extreme mental torment you are enduring. A drug, whether prescription or recreational, is still a drug, and it helps to keep the portals *open* in the auric skin that surrounds your luminous energy field, so using drugs of any kind can prolong your addiction or depression.

The best any prescription drug can do is help you cope with the invasion that is in process in your mind, but medicine cannot touch or remove the invaders. Medicine goes into your body. The invaders are *not* in your body and *not* in your brain; they have invaded your mind—your mental space. Your brain is an organ in your body. Your mind is *not* an organ in your body. The mind is your connection to your spiritual energy where your thoughts form. When you look inward, it is immense like the sky at night, and it would not fit into a brain.

DEMONS INVADE

THE MENTAL SPIRIT SPACE

WHERE YOUR WORDS FORM.

ONLY LOVING WORDS

YOU THINK ABOUT YOUR-SELF

CAN ENTER YOUR MIND

TO HEAL YOU.

THINKING "I LOVE MY-SELF"

IS THE BEST MEDICINE

YOU WILL EVER TAKE.

Most of us are not taught as children that our mental attitudes, either positive or negative, reflect on the body as our health, so when we are sick, we may feel that we are the victims of circumstances that we have no control over, but we are now looking at *our own negative attitudes as the cause of all illnesses* with amazing results. We know that negative attitudes are loaded with feelings, and your negative feelings can reflect on your body as illness.

To recover from alcoholism, drug addiction, or mental illness, you must consciously choose to entertain the attitude of positive love and goodness toward yourself and others at all times in every thought you think and every action you take, and work diligently to achieve that goal. Most people believe they can think or say anything they want to and it won't hurt them. This is not true. If you dwell mostly on negative thoughts, especially about yourself, you will create negative experiences in your life.

YOUR THINKING CAUSES

YOUR EXPERIENCE.

If you drink, use drugs, and hate yourself, the demons will invade your mental space, take control of your thoughts, and they will *add* negative words to your thinking to control your behavior. Then later on, you wonder why you have commited heinous acts that you would not ordinarily have commited. They also encourage you to kill yourself. Many people die by their own hand every day.

When demons possess your mind, they may use your body to perform mass murders in "Batman" movies, churches, and in our public schools, such as Sandy Hook Elementary School in Newtown, Connecticut. Then we blame it on guns (something visible) and send anger toward the NRA (National Rifle Association), because we are not suspecting an invisible enemy that feeds on our own self-hatred. This is commonplace in our world today. Now the invaders are using our bodies in cars to crash into crowds of people, and undoubtedly, they are hoping for nuclear war. The on-going wars on earth will never be over until at least 51 percent of the population on earth thinks Self-Love more than Self-hatred. The majority rules. Love creates Light. Hate creates darkness.

Unfortunately, anything science cannot see looking outward with their microscopes, MRI's, and X rays is just a theory (no matter how many murders are ever committed). Of course, anyone suggesting that "demons did it" would be laughed at and called crazy by people with closed minds, so nothing meaningful is accomplished or changed, and the demons go right on killing us. Most "normal" people are not paying attention to the problem anyway, in spite of millions of dysfunctional people among us. People in high government positions who probably could make a difference aren't trained to read spiritual energy and may not understand it. Along with science, they think seeing is believing, but our invisible enemy can only be seen by looking inward, and science doesn't do that (that's woo-woo!), so no progress is being made at all toward ending the killings. This is the world we live in, and this scenario has gone on around us for centuries.

The *Book of Enoch* is an ancient scriptural work written before the third century B.C. that tracks antiquity back to the first hint of corruption upon a pristine earth. This book was banned from the Old Testament and from the Hebrew Bible by the early church fathers, but it is part of the *Dead Sea Scrolls* discovered around

1945 in Qumran, which proves that the *Book of Enoch* was in existence before the time of Christ. It speaks from that obscure realm where history and mythology overlap.

According to the *Book of Enoch*, the origin of sin was rooted in the angels who fell from heaven, rather than from the Fall in the Garden of Eden. The main subject of Enoch's prophecy relates to The Watchers, evil angels who were cast out of heaven and stripped of the Auric Light (the Light that identifies spirit beings as representatives of goodness), because of their lust for the women of earth. The chief evil angel caused 200 angels to bind themselves with a horrific curse, and with him they descended to earth and mated with the daughters of men. Their progeny was a race of man-eating evil giants who were destroyed by the Great Flood, and evil spirits who continue to invade our auric field and influence our thinking on earth to this day.

Elizabeth Claire Prophet says, "fallen angels known as the Watchers, together with the progeny of the Nephilim, who were cast out of heaven by Michael the Archangel, have continued to embody on earth without interruption for at least half a million years." Now the evil spirits invade our individual auric field whenever our portals are open (due to self-hatred, drugs, or alcohol) to feed on our auric light energy like parasites and torment us until we commit suicide or die in some other tragic way (which millions of us have done).

Prophet says, "The fallen angels taught their women sorcery, incantations, and divination. They taught men every species of iniquity, including how to make swords, knives, shields, breastplates, and other instruments of war."

We live in a spiritual universe, no matter how hard we try to ignore it. How much longer will our scientists, our doctors, the people in power, and other enlightened intelligent people on earth ignore what the evil spirits are doing to us? This is not a fairytale. We cannot go on living in ignorance any longer. As Like Attracts Like, so the level to which any man has descended in consciousness is a magnet for any consciousness vibrating at the same low level.

Beholding your-Self and others in Love and spiritual perfection through Self-Awareness is the *only* way to elevate your consciousness to a higher level where evil spirits cannot enter your auric field and attack you with your death (by suicide) as their intent. We do not suspect our addictions or depression to be from a mental invasion caused by the negative way we think about our-Self or by our failure to recognize the Self as anything significant.

S.E.L.F. is an acronym for *Scientifically Evolving Life Force.* Made of Spirit Energy, *we*, as GodSpirits, are the most magnificent beings in existence, and we treat ourselves so badly in our Self-talk that we create our own hell to live in.

YOUR THINKING CAUSES

SPIRITUAL ENERGY TO MOVE.

From experience, I know that demons are translucent like clouds, even ghost-like in appearance. They come in many shapes (just as we do), and they plan treacherous plots to terrorize and torment you relentlessly. When they are controlling your mind and body, they manipulate your inner visions and raise the volume of your inner voice to loud, even blaring. They know what terrifies you, because they can read your mind, so they play on it. They take control of your thoughts and use your body to perform heinous acts against other people, and use your mouth to speak hateful words to people who love you. They destroy your relationships. They invade the chambers of your soul. They hide in your blind spots (like while driving a car), because they know you never look inward into the mental space behind your eyeballs.

They use your children to do their killing in schools and homes. They have killed zillions of us over the centuries. They cause the wars where we kill each other and encourage us to kill ourselves. Millions of us commit suicide every year.

The demons' goal is to capture and control enough mental territory so that evil and darkness will reign on earth. They cannot live in the Light. Through recessions and years of war, they have been making headway, but there are thousands of us learning to brighten our auric light by constantly thinking and filling ourselves with Self-Love and Self-Praise, which is our *best defense* against their invasion. The demons represent the direct opposite of what we are supposed to support—*love and goodness in every thought we think, especially about our-Self.* Only the quality and quantity of your Love for your-Self prevents these assassins from penetrating your luminous energy field right now.

HATING YOURSELF

CREATES MENTAL TORMENT.

LOVING YOURSELF

CREATES MENTAL PEACE.

When we watch videos showing the universe, we can clearly see both light energy and dark energy in space. Each kind of energy has living beings that represent that energy. Each kind of being lives in the same universal mental space, some representing the Light, some representing the dark. We, as Spirit-Beings, represent positive Light Energy, with our beautiful auric light shining from us. The evil spirits, who have lost their auric light, know that we are the GodSpirits, otherwise they would not spend so much time and effort invading and killing us. How many centuries will it take for us to know who we are?

We don't know yet how this Battle of the Spirits will end, but you are playing your part in this conflict with every thought you think. If you swear at yourself and call yourself names, you are supporting the negative and keeping yourself open to invasion. If you choose to support positive love and goodness toward your-Self and others across the board, then your urge to drink or use drugs will gradually disappear, and you will get well and help to heal this world.

When 51 percent or more of the people on earth collectively brighten their auric light by Loving the Self, the positive shift on earth will happen. Until then, we will continue to experience the on-going battle of good against evil. We must choose to support love and goodness individually and collectively to enable Love and Peace on earth to manifest.

I did not learn what I have shared with you here from reading a book or taking a class. I write from first-hand experience. After I saw the evil spirits in my mind by looking inward, it was just a matter of deductive reasoning to figure out how to get rid of them, and I succeeded completely. Now, as a graduate of The Four Winds Society, I am a practicing Shaman and Spiritual Teacher. During treatments, I extract demons from my clients' soul chambers in Soul Retrievals, and I work to educate people as to the cause of dysfunction on earth.

We can turn this dilemma around, but not if we go on in the same old ways that are failing. You will help to save the lives of millions of tormented people on earth who will otherwise die if you do your part to LOVE YOUR-SELF and SPREAD THE WORD.

Chapter Two

ATTITUDE IS EVERYTHING

You may find it difficult to believe the truth of what I have written here, even though there are millions of people on earth demonstrating the ill effects of the negative unseen forces in this world. During my illness, looking inward to see what was going on in my mind was the only logical thing left to do, and it worked perfectly. I could see exactly what was happening to cause so much mental disturbance. By looking outward into the world, you only see the destruction and pain the evil spirits are causing. Closing your eyes to go to sleep is a natural thing to do, but we're not trained to look inward consciously. If we were trained as children to look inward, we would not have so many problems as adults.

Some people might ask, are these demonic beings *real*? Well! Are we *really* having a chronic opioid crisis on earth? Are there *really* thousands of people in mental institutions? Are our children *really* being killed in schools by people being mentally controlled by invisible beings? Our scientists believe that "seeing is

21

NANCY LYNNE HARRIS M.A.

believing." Unfortunately, this belief hinders spiritual truth probably more than any other belief on earth. To the mentally ill person, the intrusion going on in his mind is the most real thing there is because it is so debilitating, so why waste time wondering what is *real?* We tend to not take seriously and not believe the things we cannot see by looking outward. This is a *grave* mistake.

After I recovered from depression, I did some research on the meaning of the word "conceit," since my mother had said 'loving yourself is conceited.' According to *Webster's Dictionary, conceit* means, "Endowed with intelligence and imagination, favorably minded, thinking, mental activity, high estimation, ingenious, aptitude, discernment, originality, and resourcefulness." Synonyms are "clever, idea, concept, judgment, self-love, understand, self-esteem, and admiration." The opposite word, *conceitless,* means "lack of understanding." A synonym for *conceitless* is "ignorance."

You know there are zillions of creatures that live in physical space—on, under, and above the earth. It is logical to believe that there are also other beings besides ourselves who live in inner mental space where we do our thinking. That is where the demonic beings who attack us reside. It is time for us to take back our power as the Divine Creators we are and turn on our Self-Love.

LEARNING TO LOOK INWARD

Close your eyes in a dark room or in a closet. Wait about three minutes for your vision to adjust. Then begin to look inward as if you are watching a dream. In the beginning you may see what looks like the sky at night with stars twinkling in the darkness of your mind. Then visions may begin to appear. Just watch whatever appears without imagining anything in the beginning. Practice this often to learn how to see looking inward.

As a special exercise, whenever you have an illness or a pain in your body, and you want to know what is causing it, go into a dark closet, close your eyes, and ask yourself what is causing your pain. Watch your inner screen to see the negative word that will appear on the screen or surface of your mind in answer to your question. The negative word that appears is your negative feeling (which is your attitude toward someone or something) that is causing your pain. To heal your illness, use a thesaurus to find the *exactly* opposite word, and think this new positive word without ceasing. Remember, all you're doing here is shifting the spiritual energy that controls your body from negative to positive to heal your pain or illness. When you have thought your new positive word at least 51 percent of the volume or capacity of the energy you control (whatever that is), your illness will automatically shift, and you will be well. This method will heal any illness if you think the right positive word. You control the creative energy you are made of with your own thinking all the time without realizing it. To heal myself of depression, I had to think "I love myself" 51 percent of the time to shift my mental energy to wellness. This took me about 8 months because I was very sick.

Our collective thoughts are creating our world. Each moment we individually have a choice, and a vital responsibility in our choice, of what and how to *think*. Currently, most people just let their thoughts roll/flow without paying much attention to the quality of their thinking. We can create heaven in our lives, or we can create hell, depending on the words we choose to think individually, especially about our-Self, one thought at a time.

Thinking is like traveling on a straight and narrow mental path that only goes in two directions. If we take the right path by thinking mostly positive loving words, we experience health, wealth, and many blessings along the way. But, if we take the wrong path by thinking mostly negative unloving words, we experience illness, poverty, and dysfunction, and unseen demonic beings invade our mind. This is true for everyone on this earth. The thoughts you think about your-Self are the most important thoughts of all. So, believe in your-Self as Powerful, because you are.

When you're trying to heat a cold room, you turn on the heat intentionally. If you turn off the heat, the cold comes back in. When you're trying to drive demons out of your mental space, you must think Self-Love daily without ceasing for the rest of your life. If you ever think Self-hatred more than you think Self-Love, you invite the demons back into your mental space. Demons live in the dark, so turn up the Light. Thinking Love for Your-Self lights up your mental space so invaders cannot enter your auric field.

The ability to think is such a privilege and such a misunderstood art. We create constantly with our thoughts. We are made of pure spirit energy that we can mold into love, greatness, and beauty to keep ourselves full of Light, or we can concentrate on hate, death, and destruction, individually as well as collectively, to create whatever we see manifesting around us on earth. Because *our thinking causes*, and because for centuries we have not understood this, we are dealing with much havoc in our personal lives, as well as in our world.

Our habit is to do things in a physical way (take a pill) rather than in a mental way (change a thought). We have a lot to learn about how to operate our-Self. To recover from dysfunction and to improve your life in every way, you must *watch* what you are thinking constantly, including your beliefs, and no longer just let your thoughts roll through your mind unobserved. Do you know what you just thought? Was it negative? Was it positive? You are creating your own life experience, and you can create a better life for your-Self, if you learn to change and improve your way of thinking with constant Self-correction and improvement. Aim to think in perfect positives with no fault finding and no complaining—ever. You have to constantly monitor your own thoughts.

On a scale of zero to 100 percent, how many of your thoughts are positive and how many of your thoughts are negative? Do you know? Fifty-one percent positive (out of a possibility of 100 percent) is barely enough to make a difference in your health. What are the problem areas in your life? We all know what our problems are because we think about them a lot. Dwelling on your negative feelings can cause illness to manifest in your body. Are you aware that your negative thinking causes your body to reflect as illness? You can say NO to anything, even to your own thought.

Your body is like a thermometer registering your positive and negative thoughts perfectly. Some of your pains and problems are caused from your habits of thinking negatively, and some of your pains may be caused from your past life experiences and negative patterns that are still attached to your auric field. These negative patterns can be cleaned out by an energy healer. After a cleaning, it is important that you concentrate on positive thoughts, especially about your-Self, so you do not reload your auric field with the same old problems. To reverse your negative feelings to positives, you may have to make dramatic changes in your life. Mostly positive thinking is the way to achieve excellent health. While you say and think positive words, also take positive actions to help reverse whatever you feel so negative about. Work for change and improvement in your life in every way you can.

Unfortunately, we are taught that when we are sick, someone else will heal us. We do not think about the negative things we have been concentrating on as the cause of our physical pain or illness. We tend to believe that we have no control over what happens in our body, and our illnesses just mysteriously appear. Nothing could be farther from the truth. We must take responsibility for our own negative attitudes. Your body and your mental condition are always reflecting your positive or negative attitudes, especially about your-Self.

You can make a list of the problem areas in your life and consider what you can change or do differently that will improve each area. Your choice to watch, change, and improve your way of thinking every moment of the day is the wisest choice you can make to take care of your-Self and keep your mind and body in a state of health.

Stop thinking anything negative about your-Self. You have already tried that, and you know what that has led to. If you strive to *see perfection* in your-Self, as well as in others, and to *send* Love inward to your-Self every day, as well as outward to others, you will be blessed in ways you cannot even imagine. Love your-Self as your neighbor. Loving your-Self is always your best protection from any kind of mental turmoil. Remember, if you haven't gotten well, you haven't thought enough Love for your-Self. Self-Love is your greatest protection from demonic invasion.

We misuse our thoughts because we fail to understand how powerful we are. Collectively, *we* control the winds and the waves (the weather) according to Jesus, but we need to master the Self first. If 51 percent of the people on earth began to love themselves, we would begin to experience peace on earth. Dysfunction can disappear if you are willing to change and to persevere in correcting the way you think about your beautiful magnificent *Self*. Peace of mind begins with your own *Self-Love*.

HEALING MENTAL INVASION

1. PROTECT YOURSELF - USE YOUR EYES TO LOOK INWARD OFTEN.

If invaders have violated your space, you can see them if you look quickly. They are ethereal, transparent and cloud-like, and they do not want to be seen. They are completely evil and will torment you until you commit suicide. You can see their eyes looking back at you before they hide in the shadows of your mind.

2. LOVE YOUR ENEMIES.

Send love to the evil spirits in your mental space to drive them out. They cannot live in an atmosphere of love. Say,

I SEND LOVE TO THE EVIL SPIRITS IN MY MENTAL SPACE. GET OUT! THIS IS MY SPACE!

3. LOVE YOURSELF.

The amount of Love, or God-consciousness, you have for your-Self determines whether or not evil spirits can enter your mental space. The word LOVE held in your mind will stop the course of mental invasion, but Self-Love will drive the invaders out of your mental space. Say, I LOVE YOU, (your name) often.

4. PRAISE YOURSELF.

Self-Praise is the greatest protection you can give yourself. Praise yourself for noticing every little thing that you can improve and think better. Say, "GOOD FOR ME," often. The object is to get Self-Love and Self-Praise rolling in your deep mind when you are not thinking about them so they will always protect you. Say, I PRAISE MYSELF.

GOOD FOR ME.

5. RETRAIN YOUR NEGATIVE SELF-TALK.

Always monitor what you are thinking. Tell your negative inner voice that you do not answer to what it just called you. Then tell it an endearing name it may call you. If the voice says anything objectionable to you, just *add* NO MORE to that thought, so you instantly reverse the negative thought to positive. Call yourself by an endearing name now.

6. BELIEVE IN YOURSELF AS BECOMING GREATER EVERY DAY.

Jesus made himself equal with God. He could manifest anything instantly by commanding energy perfectly. We can learn to do this too. I BELIEVE IN MYSELF.

7. **GIVE YOURSELF PERMISSION TO CHANGE.**
   Healing requires Self-correction. You have experienced what negative thinking has done for you. Reverse all your negative words to positives. I AM WILLING TO IMPROVE MYSELF. I CAN CHANGE.

8. **FORGIVE EVERYONE.**
   Do not harbor the negatives. Let it go. Move on.

9. **LIVE IN PEACE WITH YOURSELF.**
   No fault-finding. Fault-finding reflects on your own body as faults. This means no swearing, yelling, kicking, hitting, ripping, stabbing or otherwise mentally abusing yourself in your Self-talk. Peace and stillness is your mental goal. Self-persecution and Self-destruction must stop.

10. **TEACH YOUR CHILDREN TO LOVE THEMSELVES WHILE THEY ARE YOUNG.**
    Teach your little children to love themselves. You may prevent them from becoming dysfunctional as adults, and you may save their lives. Self-Love and Self-Praise are the greatest protectors of all.

11. **SAVE A FRIEND.** Tell her (him) to love herself.

12. REMEMBER THAT YOUR THINKING CAUSES.

Jesus said, "The Father and I are One." The Father IS the
Creative Light Energy that *you are made of.*
St. John said, "The Word *was* God." (and it still is!)
Your Words Create Your Life.

LOVING YOUR

S. E. L. F.

Scientifically Evolving Life Force

I consciously recognize my-Self (with a capital S)
I am an entity worth loving.
I believe in my-Self. *(This is immensely powerful.)*
I love and appreciate my-Self.
I see perfection in my-Self and in others
(No fault-finding)
I live in peace with my-Self.
I have faith in the creative power of my thought.
I can overcome anything if I change my mind.
I can change my mind. *(I do it all the time.)*
I have divine Self-worth.
I am a precious treasure, a divine being.
I have integrity.
I love my-Self as a magnificent being of Light.
I respect my-Self.
I praise my-Self for every little thing.
I deserve the best of everything life has to offer.
I refuse to worry because it improves nothing.
I am encircled and protected by Divine White Light.
I let my Light So Shine.

HEALING AFFIRMATIONS

My thinking causes.

Every day in every way my life gets better.

I treat myself sweet, kind, and loving.

I can always change my mind from negative to positive.

I treat myself like the dearest, most cherished person
I will ever know.

I *add* positive words to my mind on purpose every
minute of every day.

I am blessed.

I am the luckiest person in the whole world.

I think in a positive way to create positive experiences in
my life.

I am of the highest quality as a living, thinking being.

I love and praise myself as a divine spirit being.

I am grateful for every good thing in my life.

My burden is Light Energy controlled by my own
feelings and attitudes.

As Light Energy, I can change and create a better life.

I am powerful.

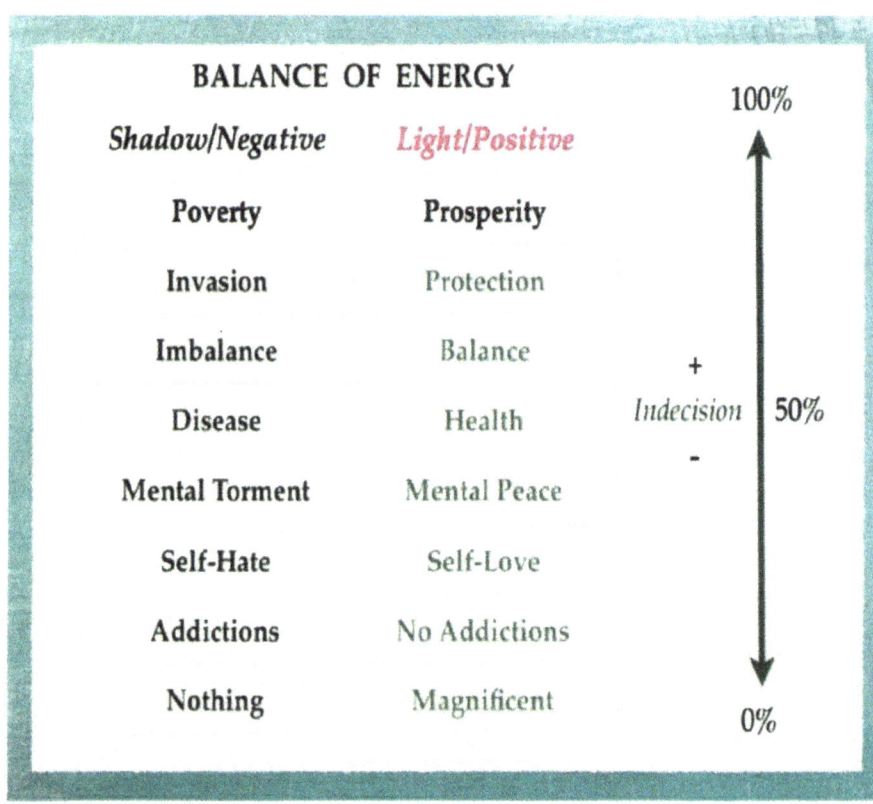

Balance of Energy Chart

ENDNOTES

1. James Van Praagh, *Ghosts Among Us: Uncovering the Truth About the Other Side* (New York: HarperCollins Publishers, 2008)141
   support@vanpraagh.com

2. Elizabeth Clare Prophet, *Fallen Angels Among Us: What You Need to Know* (Gardiner, Montana: Summit University Press, 63 Summit Way, 2010)
   4-7, 9-11, 13, www.summituniversitypress.com

3. Michael Wise, Martin Abegg Jr.,, Edward Cook, *The Dead Sea Scrolls* (New York: HarperCollins Publishers, 2005) 280-281

Also by:

NANCY LYNNE HARRIS:

MIRACLES MASTER THE ART:

Healing Medically Incurable Illness

HEAL YOURSELF OF ANYTHING

EXAMPLE GLAUCOMA

CD also available

CONSCIOUSLY OVERCOME

MENTAL ILLNESS

2-CD set also available

ABOUT THE AUTHOR

Nancy Lynne Harris, M.A., shaman and spiritual teacher, is the founder of GodSpirits United, LLC, a company that helps people recover from medically incurable illnesses and addictions by teaching them how to shift their energy for healing. She offers Books and CDs, Shamanic Illuminations, Soul Retrievals, 7 Chakra Illuminations, and Spiritual Counseling by telephone or Skype. Nancy is a graduate of The Four Winds Society, founded by Dr. Alberto Villoldo, and has also studied with Don Oscar Miro-Quesada and James VanPraagh. She graduated as a Spiritual Teacher from the Eschatology Foundation in Los Angeles.

https://www.youtube.com/watch?v=7Me7ho5Thro

https://www.youtube.com/watch?v=ci2AhHMvvK8

http://www.NancyLynneHarris.com